Preparing Our Kids for Digital Immersion

Why It's So Important to Educate Kids About Coding, Cybersecurity, Online Predators, and Cyberbullying

D1516829

Bjorn Beam

Preparing Our Kids for Digital Immersion

ISBN: 978-1-7096740-6-8   (Paperback)

First printing edition 2019.

www.SecuritySquad.org

Table of Contents

Introduction

It's no secret that our world has grown increasingly digital, from social media, texts, and messaging apps to the very state of the labor market and available job opportunities. Technology is streamlining everything we do, from how we communicate to how we manage our daily lives. Our interactions are quicker, yet more anonymous and without face-to-face contact.

As a kid growing up, if I wanted to play a game with a friend, we had to sit in the same room to play against each other over Gameboys or the classic Nintendo console system. However, that has all changed with the current generation of kids. Kids are addicted to modern cyber communication. In their minds, if they're locked away in their rooms after school, it is not isolation because they are online liking pictures, sharing content, and maintaining some form of connection with other kids. That's probably why one study found that kids spend about twenty-three hours per week on their phones—which in many families is more time than they spend with their parents.

Many kids are aware they are spending too much time on their phones. In a recent Pew Research poll, nine of out ten participants between the ages of thirteen and seventeen claimed it's the biggest problem facing their generation.

Kids, whether they are seven or fifteen, can't seem to step away from their cellular devices.

In this book, I make a case for why we need to accept the arrival of this digital age. Instead of hoping it will go away or figuring out ways to mitigate screen time, I propose a different strategy. We should focus on proper education about the dangers and exposure young people face through internet usage. Furthermore, if you depend only on pushing away technology and using parental apps, everyone will be left worse off as kids can easily circumvent these tools. They will find themselves wandering the internet unprepared while you think everything is fine. This is not security, this is insecurity.

Realistically, online predators, cyberhackers, and cyberbullies are not going away anytime soon. They are all-natural byproducts of the human mind—these people just happen to have the internet at their fingertips today and are choosing to use it for the wrong reasons. There will always be a segment of the human population that is malicious.

So if we want our kids to be prepared to deal with the current state of the world, then we need to pull back the wizard's curtain and show them the reality they live in. With the right education and a community supporting kids in the face of online transgressions, our children will be prepared to safeguard themselves, their information, and their emotions.

I am writing this book as not only a former Central Intelligence Agency (CIA) Officer and the creator of the educational startup Security Squad, but also as a concerned citizen. Technology is here to stay. It's time we reframe how we approach these topics.

Preparing Our Kids for Digital Immersion

My educational startup, Security Squad, is focused on changing the conversation surrounding digital access for kids today. In this book, we are going to first look at how our education systems massively fail kids concerning both the good and bad sides of technology in our world.

After that, we are going to get into the five major digital encounters that every child faces: cybersecurity, cyberbullying, social media interactions, online predators, and lastly, coding. With regard to coding, a tool to further prepare kids in a digital world, I make the claim that this highly sought-after skill should be more readily available in schools.

We will then look at seven reasons why kids need to be educated on digital topics immediately. Finally, I am going to propose a redefined mindset, one that is receptive yet cautious of what the world looks like today.

Don't let your child be a sitting duck—actually a sitting duckling—in the digital world. The average age at which a child receives a smartphone today is ten—yes, it is happening this early. However, even if you withhold the smartphone from your child, they are going to use their friends' and participate in the same antics. It's important to remember when you were an adolescent and all of the mischief you got yourself into. Kids are still the same today. In fact, they are even more advanced, handily circumventing security apps and settings designed to limit their screen time and phone use. If you think these parental controls are the answer, they are not—they are only Band-Aids that do not address the bigger problem.

We need to get ahead of the curve. It's time to stop dragging our heels in the sand. Smartphones are ubiquitous, social media is ingrained in our society, and people will always try to leverage new tools for bad reasons. It's time to get your family prepared.

Let's begin.

CHAPTER 1

The Current State of Our Education System

"Kids need to learn about cybersecurity, but teachers only have so much time in the day." This was a real headline published on the academic news website theconversation.com in February 2019. It perfectly encapsulates our country's problem with digital immersion: our education systems do not see cybersecurity education as paramount.

School systems still focus on traditional curriculum like mathematics, algebra, trigonometry, and three years of world history come before the safeguarding of one's personal information and identity. Don't get me wrong; I am not saying kids shouldn't learn about history or math. They are, of course, very important subjects. What I am saying is that topics like cybersecurity should be regarded as equally important during the school day.

Sadly, there are dozens of news articles across the internet lamenting the fact that most of our schools do not teach computer science (CS) today. Even worse, they do not have afterschool groups centered around dealing with cyberbullying, social media interactions, or predators, who are growing more prevalent with the availability of technology today. When I was a student, I was lucky we had a teacher that knew coding and taught it in our shop class. There is nothing like learning coding and web design with a power saw sitting next to the mouse.

Through a practice known as *sextortion*, individuals with a penchant for children are having greater success luring kids to their homes or other secluded areas through the act of *catfishing* or *masquerading* (pretending to be someone they are not to win the affection of the child/teen). We should not forget sextortion even happens among teens, whether they are the same age, or one of them is a couple of grades higher.

But before I dive into the other elements of digital immersion, let's look briefly at how our higher education systems are failing to prepare students for the state of the market today.

Higher Education: Shortage of Computer Science Education

Our education system is not just failing students at younger ages; it is also failing them as they prepare themselves for employment when they get out of college.

For instance, the number of open computer science jobs in the US continues to swell. The demand is outpacing the supply so badly that only around fifty thousand computer science graduates emerge from US universities each year, while there are an estimated five hundred thousand computer science jobs open in all major labor sectors. If you feel like doing the math, you will see that there are tens of thousands of unfilled jobs. Companies are waiting for students to walk in and claim them. The U.S. government is even incentivizing recruitment or individuals with these skills through an increase in pay and bonuses. Personally, I felt like free labor at the CIA when I had a salary conversation with my tech coworkers who received these incentives.

Now back to the topic at hand. Even worse, for the students who want to go to college for computer science degrees, there are not enough available classes or professional educators available to teach the subject. As a result, the U.S. higher education system is lagging behind those of other nations around the world.

While all of this is happening, studies show that 15 percent of college students have endured cyberbullying, while 38 percent of respondents said they know of someone who is facing cyberbullying at their institution.

So, not only are our college students not being prepared to go out into the world without student debt and to clinch an open computer science job, but they are also being preyed upon through social channels and social media profiles—a problem they might have avoided if they had been provided with this digital education.

The Same Story in K-12

Though there is a huge opportunity for computer science education in the nation's colleges and universities, the situation is just as dire for K-12 students.

Some states are trying to make a difference. In California, where only 39 percent of high schools offer computer science classes, the State Board of Education approved the California Computer Science Implementation Plan. Under the plan, computer science would be worked into other classes, and computer science courses would be available at introductory and advanced levels for every grade. But the plan is a pipe dream—the state does not have the necessary funding to make this happen. So despite the ambition of the State Board of Education, the state of computer science in California remains the same.

And the story is similar throughout the country. In the 2018 State of Computer Science Education annual report from the Code.org Advocacy Coalition and the Computer Science Teachers Association (CSTA), data showed that many states fail to offer computer science education. In Florida, just 19 percent of schools offer relevant CS courses; 32 percent offer CS in Wisconsin; 22 percent in North Dakota.

These numbers are especially troubling when you think about how frequently young students interact with digital tools and various internet functions. They're engaging with a world that they haven't been properly trained to handle, and the lack of preparation is having a negative impact.

K-12 Students, the Internet, and Mental Health

If students were armed with the CS education they needed, they would be better equipped to handle the challenges of life online. More than 71 percent of students in K–12 education classes right now are concerned about cyberbullying. Of those who have reported being cyberbullied, about 24 percent went on to confirm that they have had their private information shared online, exposing their safety, location, and personal information. With some digital know-how, perhaps they could have avoided these incidents.

An estimated 33.8 percent of students between the ages of twelve and seventeen have been victims of cyberbullying. Concerning mental health, 24 percent of these students reported having suicidal thoughts after being victims of cyberbullying. The impacts of these attacks are not felt equally—girls are 36.3 percent more likely than boys to be victims of cyberbullying campaigns.

Unfortunately, the number of victims is only increasing, signaling that something needs to be done.

Of course, there are reasons why these critical topics are not being covered in our schools today. In the next chapter, I propose why schools of all levels are resisting critically important topics and discussions with their students.

CHAPTER 2

Why the Pushback?

None of us likes to feel stupid, and that, of course, holds true for parents, teachers, and administrators. With something like technology, which has only been readily accessible to the masses for fifteen to eighteen years now, the very "adults" in charge also need the same kind of education we are proposing for children.

Despite how ubiquitous smartphones and digital culture are, not everyone knows how to use these tools or participate in the greater online conversation. An estimated 36 million adults lack digital literacy skills. In a 2016 Pew Research Center study, 52 percent of surveyed adults were "relatively hesitant" to learn digital skills. Within that group, 14 percent were completely unprepared to adopt technology into their everyday lives, 5 percent had technology but did not trust it or use it often, and 33 percent were just reluctant to learn more. Many of these adults were aged fifty or older. But even when looking at adults who are in their thirties and forties, there's still less familiarity with digital skills, despite their proximity to technology and recent developments.

Generally speaking, a lot of different adults fall into the category of being digitally naïve, but many of them are likely parents and teachers. They have a desire to be the experts in the room, but that is difficult to do when they do not have the right knowledge.

They don't want to look foolish or embarrassed in front of these technologically savvy children, so they don't broach these topics at all.

They would rather sweep these issues under the rug as opposed to admitting to their six-year-old students that they don't know how to keep their personal information private.

Here are a few other reasons why digital immersion pushback is happening across the board today:

Understanding Data

There are prerequisites that come with studying a topic like cybersecurity or coding. It's not something that can be haphazardly taught in a few after-school sessions. These are topics that require months of material, with the lessons building on one another to arrive at the desired results.

Therefore, schools do not want to get involved. It would demand a major overhaul of the current systems as well as the shifting around of time blocks and educational requirements starting as early as elementary school.

Overstretched Staff

Implementing programs to educate students about digital topics would, in many cases, overstretch teachers and staff who are currently being pushed beyond their limits. As it stands, the American school curriculum is already considered overcrowded. Thus, as I have mentioned, a major structural overhaul would have to take place to create a system where teachers are not overstretched and underequipped.

Teachers Are Not Cybersecurity Experts

The ability to teach about cybersecurity and coding can only be gained through a very specific education. Teachers who went to school for education, history, and English probably feel they have zero ability to learn and teach cybersecurity and coding. These topics require a certain technical approach to the subject matter that is different from classic education techniques. When you couple this different approach with older teachers set in an established teaching pattern, it can become that much more difficult to shift the teaching mindset.

In fact, a 2018 PricewaterhouseCoopers survey found that only 10 percent of K–12 teachers feel comfortable using "high-tech" devices. When it came to teaching computer science topics like data analytics, graphic design, programming, and engineering design, the percentage of teachers who felt capable of teaching these subjects never topped 17 percent. So, in addition to lacking the background to help students with digital immersion, teachers also lack the comfort level and interest.

One huge downside of this teaching deficiency is how students engage with technology in an educational setting. Sixty percent of the time, they are simply consuming content through tech, such as watching videos or reading articles on websites. Only 32 percent of students report active tech use, meaning coding, some form of data analysis, or creating and producing content. Without the right guidance, they become passive users who lack necessary skills and fail to unlock the true power of the tech at their fingertips.

Therefore, in order to make cybersecurity and coding part of the middle school and high school curriculum, schools will need to start hiring coding professionals that are not necessarily part of the typical teacher system.

Improving and changing information security behaviors requires more than just supplying teachers with study guides. The teachers need to be willing to learn how to apply these new behaviors in the class and at home. They may argue, "Are we being paid enough for this?" The sad answer to this question is that educators were not being paid enough before.

Parents Need to Step In

Parents are increasingly busy today. In most families, both parents need to work to pay all of the outstanding bills. Parents have also fallen victim to the digital revolution, in which their jobs follow them home after they leave the office. Therefore, they do not exactly have time to become at-home coding teachers for their kids. Parents leave the responsibility of teaching this important topic to the school system, without realizing the importance of leading by example at home.

When it comes to something like cybersecurity, parents have a lot of learning to do. They may be exposing their personal information and their children's information without even realizing it. What are their privacy settings on their social media pages where they have pictures of their kids? Are the parents changing their passwords, or do they use one simple password they have written down on the refrigerator? If children are to learn the components of cybersecurity, then parents need to be willing to educate themselves as well. Any network is only as strong as the weakest link. Improving the entire family's cybersecurity strengthens the entire network. To further demonstrate this point, my amazing parents, who are in their 60s and 70s, did not know most of the answers to the questions in my educational comic "Security Squad: Your Kid's Playbook to Cybersecurity, Cyberbullying, and Coding!" To put this in a bit more context, this book is for eight-to ten-year-olds.

But despite being the weak links in the family, many parents are not looking to external resources or experts for advice. A reported 40 percent of parents are being taught by their kids how to use their technology. If the kids do not understand the dangers of digital immersion, how can they teach their parents? Additionally, when parents do decide to intervene, it is not to educate, but rather it is to spy or reprimand. Sixty-five percent of parents take away cellphone or internet privileges as a form of punishment, 55 percent have put a limit on internet use, and more than 60 percent have checked their teen's social media profiles or browsing history. But again, without proper knowledge of the risks, how do parents know what to look for?

Parents and schools both see these obstacles as too vast and overwhelming to overcome. Instead, they continue to make the wrong moves or push everything to the wayside, hoping it will all go away or, even worse, hoping that the other party will take charge.

Well, I am here to tell you, these issues will not go away.

Monkey See, Monkey Do

Countless studies have proven that children mimic and imitate parents, teachers, and adults—to a fault. If parents are not enforcing a positive kind of digital immersion at home, and if teachers don't address it in the classrooms, then children end up alone, with a phone in their hands, connected to the good and bad world at all times.

With just the tap of a thumb, your child can talk to someone in China, release personally-identifying information to someone two neighborhoods away, and disclose their address to a predator pretending to be a twelve-year-old girl in an Instagram direct message.

We all need to wake up to the realities of the digital world. Your child will mimic you and do what you tell them to do. That is why you need to be on board with this new kind of mindset. We need to redefine how we look at child online activity, as well as the conversations surrounding it.

CHAPTER 3

Make It Known, Make It Fun

At this point, we've looked at the state of education and safety for kids ranging from preschool through college today. We have looked at why schools are resisting the necessary changes that will prepare our kids and our countries for the aggressions of the future.

But before surveying the five most important digital topics that should be at the top of every curriculum in our schools today, I am going to make a case for two things (in order for this to be successful):

1. **Make it known:** It is time to bring things out into the open and cover the five biggest digital immersion topics every kid should at least be well versed in. In the coming chapters, I am going to break down everything you need to know about these topics, as well as some of their initial background, so you can begin educating your child moving forward.

   But before diving into the specifics of *what* to cover in these conversations, it's critical to understand *how* to conduct them. First and foremost, remember that this conversation should be a dialogue, not a lecture. Ask questions about what your kids know. Give examples and check for understanding. This is an opportunity to open up the channels of communication and act as a partner to your child or student, not just an enforcer. Furthermore, these types of back-and-forth discussions can boost children's brain response to language. Not only are you making kids smarter about using the internet, but you're also improving their language and conversation skills.

It is also important to let your kids know that the conversation is a safe space. You might find out that they have engaged in behavior that put them at risk. This is not the time to scold or punish; this is the time to teach them about why those behaviors were risky and how to avoid them in the future. Encourage them to think critically about their actions online, and be sure to give context for the things you are discussing. For example, if you tell your child they should not accept gifts from strangers online, explain why. Think of the conversation as a way to protect them in the future.

If you start to make these discussions a regular occurrence in your household, you will remove the "taboo" labeling that can, in many cases, make kids want to rebel even more. Make it known what happens in the world (with sensitivity to the age of your child, of course). There is no need to sound the alarm bells and cause panic.

2. **Make it fun:** Toward the end of this book, I am going to explore the topic of *gamification*, which is essentially the act of turning an academic activity like reading or coding into a game. It means adding game-like qualities to something while disguising the actual helpful and educational components of the content. Many app developers are doing this in their travel or social media apps today, as gamification has proven to get people more involved and interested in a topic. Furthermore, gamification is becoming a bigger part of all our lives, whether it is through the awards you get in your Duolingo app for making it to the next level or the awards an Uber driver collects for his/her rides. However, it is important to note that gamification does not need to be high tech. When you told your kids to pretend that the spoonful of peas was a flying

airplane coming in for a landing in their mouth, you demonstrated the fun and creative skill of gamification.

Overall, gamification is relevant because an estimated 97 percent of kids play video games. When you make learning about digital topics fun, you are speaking their language. Friendly competition helps, too—60 percent of learners report that seeing leaderboards motivates them to participate and perform at a higher level. And teachers have seen the benefits. Seventy percent of teachers report seeing increased engagement among students when educational video games are introduced. In short, gamifying learning can only produce positive results.

At the end of the day, it is important to remember we are dealing with kids. We should not approach them with a doomsday mindset. This will give them anxiety. Instead, we should accept the realities of what they need to learn and make it fun. Yes, it is possible to learn about cybersecurity and coding and make your kids laugh and enjoy themselves at the same time.

With this in mind, it is now time to foray into the five topics we have been discussing: cybersecurity, cyberbullying, social media interactions, online predators, and coding.

CHAPTER 4

Cybersecurity

One single vulnerability is all an attacker needs.
—Window Snyder

With the convenience of having everything you could ever want in the palm of your hands comes the big responsibility of safeguarding your personal and financial information. Each time you surrender your credit card information to a site or your address to a social media platform, you are exposing yourself and your security to outside forces. This is where we all think it starts since we tend to think about our banking and credit card information first and foremost in cybersecurity. But from the moment you click on a website, you are exposing yourself and your data to outside forces through cookies and other stealth technology that may be connected to that website and lead to loss or exposure of personal data.

It's a gamble we all take every single day.

The problem is that cyberattackers are growing more sophisticated by the day in their hacking abilities. A cyberattacker in 2020 compared to one in 2001 is a completely different beast. These attackers are wreaking havoc on individuals, kids, and companies alike. Over $45 billion was spent on managing cyberattacks in the year 2018 alone.

In order to stop these attackers, we need to invest in cybersecurity education. If you know your enemy, you can stop them before they draw their weapon. Instead of remaining on the defensive, hoping you will go unnoticed, you can take an offensive stance with information and education. Starting early and educating often is the best way to build awareness in childhood education.

6 Ways Cyberattackers Can Steal Your Information:

1. **Phishing:**

   Phishing is another word for a fake email masquerading as a legitimate one. Although kids ages three through nine probably won't be using email, kids over the age of ten will. (Many schools send out emails to alert students of closings, delays, etc.) Hackers create these phishing emails with the intent of stealing personal information, like passwords, bank account information, and social security numbers.

   Phishing emails try to appear like they came from a well-known person or organization that would likely be reaching out (e.g., a nonprofit offering a student a grant or scholarship). The emails try to instill a sense of urgency: "Act now or the offer will be gone tomorrow." But no legitimate email from an institution will put pressure on you to answer in four hours. That is your first clue it's a phishing email.

   The phishing email will also contain some kind of link that makes it easy for the recipient to input credit card details immediately. The phishers aren't going to beat around the bush. There could be an attachment with a virus in the email as well. Tread cautiously.

   Additionally, look at where the email came from. If the email is cindy@bankofamerica.com, it's probably legitimate. But if the email is cindy@banksoftheamericas.com, it's clearly someone trying to pretend they work with the bank.

Phishing emails are often riddled with spelling mistakes since many of them are generated by hackers in foreign countries. If you see spelling mistakes or strange phrasing, it is probably a sign of malicious intent.

Lastly, the most important part is to trust your instincts—if something does not seem right, it probably isn't. Do not open unknown or suspicious emails, and do not forward them. If you have a question about authenticity, find authentic contact information on the internet and contact the provider directly. Notifying them may allow them to take precautions to reduce the damage of a phishing email campaign.

2. **Malware:**

Malware is another word for malicious software that was created to compromise a system and steal data from it. Malware, among other bad things, can modify a system's core functionalities and track a victim's activities long after they have been downloaded. Major types of malware include the following:

- Viruses: Even if you do not consider yourself digitally savvy, you have likely heard of computer viruses. A virus is a malicious code or program that was written for the specific purpose of changing the way a computer operates. It latches on to a document or program and then spreads from one system to another. Among the many things viruses can do, they can corrupt and destroy important data.

- Trojans: A Trojan horse, better known as a Trojan, is malicious code or software that's designed to look trustworthy. You might be tricked into downloading a Trojan because it seems legitimate, but once it's on your computer, it can damage your system and steal information.

- Spyware: Spyware is malicious software that tracks and stores your personal information and sends it to a third party (e.g., advertisers, data firms, bad actors, etc.). Spyware can track your passwords, monitor your activity, and spy on sensitive information you share on your computer. The information retrieved through spyware can be used for identity theft and other forms of cybercrime.

- Keyloggers: Keylogger is short for keystroke logger. This is a software program that tracks every key you strike on your keyboard. Essentially, every action you take on your device is watched, with the intent of using it against you. The objective is to collect sensitive information, like your passwords and credit card numbers. Keyloggers are an especially serious threat because they're so covert and provide unprecedented access to your digital activity.

Regardless of the type of malware that you're up against, it is the last thing you want to deal with on a laptop or computer.

To stay safe, be sure to have antivirus software downloaded on your kid's computer. Encourage them never to download any unknown software or click on any software pop-ups that appear on weird websites (many kids end up on weird meme sites). Furthermore, having the software is not enough. Make sure you frequently update the software and run antivirus scans to detect any malicious software on your device.

3. Mal-Apps:

Although fairly new, malicious apps or mal-apps are something your kids should look out for when downloading apps from the Google Play and App Stores. Yes, these stores work hard to vet all the apps being loaded onto them. However, there are still master hackers who manage to slip their apps through, and these apps contain malicious code that can put your personal privacy at risk.

Look out for account access, SMS permission, microphone access, and contact access requests upon downloading apps. To avoid these problems, check the permissions before downloading the app, as well as reviews and ratings. It's a good rule of thumb to tell your kid not to download any app with fewer than fifty thousand downloads. Lastly, never ever download apps from third-party app stores.

Finally, while this has been said many times before, Apple devices and software are not immune to malware and mal-apps. Anything connected to the internet is susceptible, and that includes your Internet of Things (IoT) fish tank sensor. (In 2017, hackers used a fish tank sensor at a North American casino to access the casino's data.)

4. Smishing:

Smishing is the new phishing, except it is done through SMS messaging. These texts are tricky, and if you're not paying attention, they can get you to divulge information more easily than a phishing email. Many smishers will pretend to be banks and send a link to your phone telling you your account has been hacked and that you need to reset your password.

No legitimate bank is going to ask you to reset your password through a text. They are going to call you. Additionally, you can try to call the smishing number if they are pretending to be someone you know. See where the number goes. However, as a precaution, I would advise only reaching out to your bank directly using an official number listed on its website or on your billing statement if you feel unsure.

5. **Physical Security Threats:**

There are plenty of people who have figured out how to look back out at you through phone and laptop cameras. Webcam hacks have become especially common. Although there is not much you can do about this, you can ensure your kids keep tape over their laptop cameras at all times unless they are absolutely needed. Webcam hacks typically occur through one of the methods listed above. This also includes issues with smart devices, like Alexa. So again, keep your antivirus software up to date to minimize this risk.

6. **Unsecure Networks:**

If you connect any of your systems or devices to an unsecured network, you can provide the hacker with access to all of the files on your system. As you can imagine, this can end poorly for you and your children. When a hacker ends up in control of your systems, they can steal the passwords from your social accounts and bank accounts as well as other sensitive information.

To keep this from happening, never connect to open Wi-Fi networks that you can't trust. Even if it's a free network, don't assume it's one you can trust. If you're at a café, ask for the staff Wi-Fi network and password, if possible, as opposed to the public option. Most importantly, consider getting a virtual private network (VPN). VPNs increase the security and privacy of public online connections, allowing you to access a public network as if your device were connected to a private network.

These are the six most common ways cyberattackers are infringing on your child's security today. Of course, there are many other ways they can try to infiltrate your children's lives, which is why teaching them the basics of cautious internet usage can be incredibly beneficial for your entire family's personal safety.

What Is Cybersecurity?

Cybersecurity is officially defined as "techniques that protect computers, networks, programs, and data from unauthorized access or attacks that are used for exploitation." In most cases, cybersecurity is enacted by a third-party software or company. At some companies, it's handled by an entire internal department. There are a few key types of cybersecurity:

- Application security: This is about stopping any threats to software or devices, as a compromised application puts sensitive data at risk of exposure. Strong application security is usually baked in during the design stage.

- Information security: This category of security is about keeping data private at all times, including when it's stored and when it's in transit.

- Disaster security: This is all about how an organization responds to cyberattacks. When data is already lost or systems and operations are compromised, the company needs to get back on its feet quickly, and it needs to do so while preventing any further data loss.

- Network security: Network security is about protecting computer networks from hackers and bad actors who may install malware.

- Operational security: This involves the day-to-day management and use of computer systems, including who has access and at what levels. Tight controls can help prevent data breaches and attacks.

- Education: As important as it is to put protocols and systems in place to safeguard data, it's also critical to educate the end-user. Similar to the level of information provided by this book, great cybersecurity education can help people avoid making mistakes that leave them or their organizations vulnerable. This could cover everything from recognizing suspicious emails to the use of USB flash drives.

Within each of these categories, there are several subcategories that can be covered and many specialty products that can be used for protection. As you can see, it's a pretty extensive topic, which is why it needs to be embedded in our education systems. Not to mention, given the rising importance of cybersecurity, there is a massive number of unfilled jobs related to the industry, which is why exposing kids to this way of thinking can set them up for their future.

Lastly, cybersecurity education will keep kids safe as they get older, helping them ensure their information and tech projects are as secure as possible. It's an investment in the future of our economy and GDP, and it starts with something as simple as teaching about cybersecurity.

Now that you know the basics of preparing your child for personal information attacks, it's time to look at a sad and disturbing reality in which cyberattacks undermine our mental health and emotional well-being.

CHAPTER 5

Cyberbullying

Pulling someone down will never help you reach the top.

We all know that to be true. That's why many people, including kids, will never use their phones or laptops to cyberbully. The problem is that there will always be the minority group of insecure people who are excited to be anonymous keyboard warriors and wreak havoc on students of all ages.

In the age of the internet, we also have to balance the age of the individual. One individual can wield a massive amount of power with one smartphone, making hundreds of kids feel sad, depressed, anxious, or suicidal.

The effects of cyberbullying are very real today. The Centers for Disease Control reports that suicide is among the three leading causes of death among young people, with a strong link to bullying. If there is anything to take away from this book, this chapter is arguably the most important.

You need to be aware of these terrifying statistics, so your child is prepared for the internet predators and anarchists—or to coin a phrase *predarchs*. The internet makes it easy for other kids to say nasty things—there's no longer the pressure or consequences of face-to-face contact. Weak, cowardly students can make anonymous accounts on social media sites and say whatever they want, to whomever they want. Throw in a little technological inclination, and these aggressors can virtually torture your child without you even realizing it.

It's a deadly killer that is also completely silent. In the physical world, there is no trace. That's why our students should be prepared to deal with and combat this kind of bullying, both from a self-preservation standpoint and by accessing school resources and whistleblowing systems so that they don't feel like "snitches." Furthermore, the more we understand cyberbullying, the more we can treat the root causes of the bullying itself.

First, it's important to understand the different kinds of cyberbullying that could be impacting your child today:

1. **Harassment:**

   As the most common form of cyberbullying, *harassment* involves the bully sending offensive and malicious messages to an individual or a group one or more times. When the cyberbully decides to take it one step further and threaten physical harm or send increasingly aggressive messages, cyber harassment is elevated to cyberstalking. Sometimes, this can lead to actual harm in the real, offline world, which is why it's so important that students alert staff and parents about these kinds of threats.

2. **Flaming:**

   Similar to harassment, *flaming* is cyberbullying that goes on in emails, chat rooms, or instant messaging. It is a type of public bullying that directs harsh language, images, and videos at a specific person. Flaming can be used interchangeably with harassment depending upon the situation.

3. **Exclusion:**

This is where cyberbullying starts to get hard to track. *Exclusion* is the act of intentionally singling out and removing or excluding a person from online chat groups, Facebook groups, Instagram groups, and sites. The group then targets the person that was left out, leaving them messages, sending screenshots, and making it known that they were left out of the group.

This is a common attack waged on young women and can have serious, irreversible mental effects on the victim.

4. **Outing:**

Outing has made the news recently related to LGBT students. One student in September 2019 was outed as bisexual to classmates. He then went on to take his own life. *Outing* is defined as when a bully shares personal and private information, pictures, or videos about someone publicly without that person's approval. This commonly revolves around sexual orientation, surgeries, sexual encounters, and sometimes pictures/videos of sexual activities that were filmed without the other person's consent. Additionally, the making and distribution of nude or sexual photos/videos constitutes child pornography. This makes it that much more important to stop and prevent, and it may likely require the involvement of law enforcement.

5. **Masquerading:**

Also known as *catfishing*, which is more popularly linked with online deceit in romantic relationships, *masquerading* is the process by which a bully creates a fake identity to harass someone anonymously. They can pretend to be someone else, make up the name and profile entirely, or use an anonymous, no-picture account to do it. These people can make dozens of Instagram accounts in a single day, sending the same messages over and over again to the victim even though they are being consistently blocked by the victim.

6. **Fraping:**

    Fraping can start out harmlessly yet end in major reputational damage, educational opportunities, and employment. This is when a student signs into their friend's social media account, pretends to be them, and posts racial or homophobic slurs. If the slurs are bad enough, they can go viral and potentially get the student in trouble at school. This can permanently damage their reputation.

It doesn't take a rocket scientist to know that cyberbullying has been linked to increased reports of teen depression, anxiety, and suicide. As humans, we are emotionally fragile, and even the strongest of people will feel sad and lonely if they are purposely excluded from things. A child is now not only judged by their actions in person but also by their growing archive of photos, messages, and texts on various social media platforms. There's a digital judgment that lasts a lifetime.

So how can you keep your child safe? First, share with them the common forms of cyberbullying above. Get the conversation about this topic out in the open so they are equipped to deal with it when it happens to them. If you suspect it is happening and they aren't telling you, here are some signs your child is a victim of cyberbullying:

- They appear jumpy or anxious when an email or message pops up on their phone.

- They try to call in sick to school more frequently.

- They appear angry and depressed after they are on their

mobile device.

- They are secretive about what they do on the computer, and they may get mad if you view their screen.

- They are withdrawing from friends and don't have social plans on weekends.

- They are ornery and sad all the time.

It is difficult to shield kids completely from cyberbullying today. Encourage your children to ignore the bullies, and if the bullying persists, to let you know so you can report it to the school. Block the email addresses and usernames of online bullies as efficiently as possible. Cut back on the time your child spends on the phone and computer in the first place.

Most importantly, keep an open dialogue running with your child. Refrain from punishing them for being a victim of cyberbullying. It's not their fault. Have an educational session every weekend where you go over different cyberbullying cases, so they know cyberbullying is a reality they can share with you.

Of course, during those formative teen years, angst can prevent a dialogue between you and your child. That's why there needs to be school programs or something else (e.g., Security Squad) that can prepare your child.

Finally, we should not only talk about cyberbullying from the victim's point of view. It is also important to understand the mindset of the cyberbully to tackle the problem at the root cause. First, it cannot be overstated that there are a variety of causes that lead a child to cyberbully. Therefore, it is important for parents, teachers, and school administrators to investigate each case as closely as possible. Cyberbullying often comes from someone feeling that they are in a position of weakness. This can result from family issues at home that make them feel helpless. It can also be caused by isolation at school, boredom, self-loathing, a sense of revenge, or that they themselves are sometimes victims of cyberbullying. Cyberbullying can be a way for them to regain power that they feel was lost in some other aspect of their life. Additionally, because of the feeling of distance the internet provides, cyberbullies may not actually realize the degree of harm a tweet, message, or photo can cause.

CHAPTER 6

Social Media Interactions

For many of you reading this, you didn't have a social media account until at least the age of eighteen. For older parents, you still may not have one. That is okay, but you probably have no idea what it's like for a six- or seven-year-old to engage on social media.

I know what you're probably thinking: "Well, there aren't six-year-olds on Facebook! That's silly."

Think again. According to eMarketer.com, 5.7 million children under the age of eleven have accounts on Instagram, Facebook, and Snapchat, regardless of the restrictions that keep children from using these apps.

That's how universally popular social media sites have become today. Everyone wants to get in on the action. Why? Social media taps into something so innate to human beings—the desire to belong and receive praise for one's actions, decisions, or accomplishments. We're social beings at heart, which is why humans have clustered in communities and neighborhoods since the beginning of time. We do best when we are in contact with those who are similar to us.

Adults aren't immune to the pull of social media either. You have probably engaged in your fair share of social media fights and arguments. You've probably unfriended some people over politics or ostracized a few family members. When we're positioned behind our keyboards, unfortunately, the darker side of our personality can come out to play.

Your kids need to be prepared for all of the time they spend on social media. They need to be aware that their posts and comments are not only permanent but also publicly accessible. (Yes, even private accounts—someone can take a screenshot of your post and do whatever they want with it.) Even if you have the highest privacy settings and no friend connections on your account, you are still vulnerable because the website is vulnerable. The moment anyone gets on social media, they are basically surrendering every last detail about themselves.

Social Media Interaction Basics

Social media is a big, ever-changing exchange of information and conversation between people throughout the world. There are public ways to chat on social media, like commenting on photos or sharing posts. Then there are discreet forms of communication through direct message portals, closed groups, and poll responses.

These different channels of communication can get kids in trouble if they don't know what they are doing. Let's break it down a little bit further:

1. **Public Posts Are Permanent:**

    Remember, anytime anything is posted on social media, consider it permanent for all eternity. Therefore, if your child has a private Facebook profile but still proceeds to publish something racist, there is a good chance it can come back around to haunt them.

    Posts are permanent for a number of reasons. First, anyone can take a screenshot of a post even if it's a private profile. Second, social media sites have said that all content posted therein is contained within their servers. Even if you delete it, a heinous post can still make its rounds. Third, there are systems around the world that are time archiving various versions of websites. With all of this data being collected and stored, computer programing is catching up with how to process it. *Big data*, the field of analyzing and compartmentalizing data too big or complex for traditional data processing, and *artificial intelligence* (AI) are making this data more and more usable. In the near future, job applications, college applications, and mortgage/insurance policies will likely use AI analysis of all of your kid's messages, photos, and tweets on social media to determine their stability or ability to collaborate at college, at work, and at life.

So if your kid thinks they are free to post whatever they want on social media, make sure you tell them why that is not the case, even with a private account. Their posts today could impact their chances of being accepted into a good college, getting a job, or receiving a promotion in the future. Don't believe me? This article highlights the stories of six people who were fired for their social media posts, and this is just the tip of the iceberg.

2. **Private Messages Can Be Screenshot:**

If your child thinks they are having an intimate, discreet conversation with a friend through Instagram messenger or WhatsApp, tell them to think again. This person could take screenshots and send images of the chat to anyone and everyone. Even if a channel appears like it's not public, that doesn't mean it can't become public very, very quickly.

3. **Images Can Be Screenshot:**

There is never a time when it's acceptable for a kid or teen to send provocative photos of themselves through social media. Especially with apps like Snapchat that delete the content after eight to ten seconds, because the recipient can still take a screenshot before that happens. There are even apps that circumvent Snapchat's instant delete rule, allowing the app owner to automatically store and access these photos without the other person knowing. So the "#feltcutemightdeletelater" movement doesn't really exist at all. Any content sent through social media can be captured and leveraged by the recipient, no matter how the app is set up.

4. **Texts Can Be Hurtful:**

When we type to each other, we are leaving out the inflections, intonation, and personality of our voices. This can make online messaging seem much meaner and colder than regular in-person conversations. Therefore, if your kid is in chat rooms or messaging through social media a lot, try to educate them on how to be polite and nice without the vocal intonation assistance. This type of education can also inform a potential cyberbully of how hurtful online actions can be. Helping them understand the repercussions could serve as a turning point to divert them from that type of interaction. Social media etiquette humanizes our interactions and can help us understand the hurtful nature of some texts.

5. **Predators Can Hide Behind Fake Accounts:**

Social media is becoming an increasingly popular way for online predators to get young kids and teens to send them disgusting content. They can make fake profiles in just minutes and get started connecting with profiles on Facebook and Instagram.

Basically, at the end of the day, anything we say or exchange through social media should be vetted as something we would share with a room of one hundred of our closest friends and family members. If what you are going to say or post isn't something you could say to these people, then it's probably not appropriate to share on social media.

Social media is much more permanent than most kids realize. If there's one thing to take away from this chapter, it's to show your kid how permanent all posts on social media truly are.

Plus, if your kids are putting less provocative content out into the world, they are less likely to be targets of exclusion or other forms of cyberbullying. Some things are better left private.

CHAPTER 7

Online Predators

We've arrived at a chapter that probably no parent ever wants to read. However, we all need to be vigilant, which is why the discussion of online predators can't be left to the wayside. These are real, living, breathing human beings, possibly located right in your neighborhood. The internet has provided them with a slew of tactics for reaching your children and convincing them to come over for a snack or a swim.

These bad actors are especially formidable to teens looking for a partner or someone to love them. These predators know how to make it seem like they are also fourteen or fifteen years old. It's so important that your child knows this before engaging with others on the internet.

Let's first go over some statistics.

About 95 percent of teens between twelve and seventeen are online. Of these teens, about one in five reports that they have received an unwanted sexual solicitation via the internet. These solicitations allegedly took the form of requests to engage in sexual activities or sexual talk, or to give out personal sexual information.

At the same time, 75 percent of children are willing to share personal information online about themselves and their families in exchange for goods, services, or presents. In a world that makes us all feel increasingly lonely, 33 percent of teens are also Facebook friends with people they have never met in person. Virtual pen pals have become something of the norm today.

Predators know this, which is where they slip into the equation.

Cyber predators typically fall between the ages of eighteen and fifty-five and prey on children ages eleven to fifteen. As of 2015, there were 799,041 registered sex offenders living in the US. That is just the number of those who have been caught and convicted.

How Do Online Predators Work?

Predators make it their mission to establish contact with kids through conversation. You can find them in chat rooms, instant messaging windows, email, and discussion boards. With so many peer support boards and forums today that deal with anxiety and depression, many of these predators also turn up in these chats looking for vulnerable and lonely victims.

Online predators don't work quickly or obviously, as grooming takes time. They gradually seduce their targets through comments, attention, compliments, affection, and eventually, even gifts. They do this over a significant timeline, so it can be hard to notice anything happening in the interim. You might worry because your child is playing games on a huge multiplayer platform with strangers. But what matters most is how they interact with the other players. For example, do they get free digital gifts from the other players to improve their character's skills?

Predators will also make it a point to learn about kids' trends, habits, likes, and dislikes. They will listen to the same music and go to the same movies so that they have things in common to discuss. They will be able to sympathize with the kids, winning over their trust and possibly even turning them against you, the parent. "Gosh, that is so unfair your parents are not letting you go to the mall this weekend. They do not know how to have fun."

While all of this is happening, they will try to ease young people's inhibitions by introducing sexual content into conversations. Again, they will do this gradually, although the content will ratchet up in its inappropriateness by the end (e.g., pictures and videos).

Which Kids Are at Risk?

Technically, any kid, particularly under the age of eighteen, on social media or the internet is at risk for meeting and engaging a predator. Predators know these kids are young enough not to notice anything out of the ordinary. Their innocence is something they will feed off of, using it to their advantage over time.

Predators also know that teens, specifically ages twelve to sixteen, are exploring their sexuality and newfound body parts, and looking to move away from their parents' control and rebel. In swoops the predator, ready to be a shoulder to cry on.

- Kids who are most at risk of becoming victims of online predators include the following:

- Kids who have just joined the internet and are not familiar with online etiquette

- Kids seeking affection or attention that they do not receive from parents/teachers

- Kids going through a rebellious phase

- Kids feeling isolated or lonely, potentially from the cyberbullying that goes on at their school

- Kids who are curious and confused about their sexual identity

- Kids who are naïve

As you can see, this list describes an inordinate number of kids today. Some of these attributes surely describe your kids, students, nieces, or nephews. Therefore, what can you do to keep your kid safe? You can make them aware that these predators are at large, so they are alert before any issues even happen.

Additionally, it's okay to set some ground rules in your home. As a parent or teacher, you should do the following:

- **Get involved:** Educate your kids about sexual predators. Share stories. Cover their most common tactics and messaging methods so they are aware. Do not leave kids alone to navigate the waters of the internet with no experience or guidance.

- **Say no to chat rooms:** There is no need to be in a chat room, especially with social media today. Tell your kids they can have social media (you can't shut down everything or else they will rebel), but that they can't be in chat rooms.

- **Put computers in public spaces:** Do not let a child who's just eleven years old have a private computer in their bedroom. Keep it in a visible communal space.

- **Share email addresses:** When a kid is young (younger than fifteen or sixteen), use just one email for the family.

- **Rules about internet friends:** Instead of telling your child they are not allowed to have internet friends (this will never work and will only make them angry), tell them about the rules. Kids should not be meeting these internet friends in person because of the various safety reasons we have discussed.

- **Keep open communication:** Make sure you make it clear that your child can come to you at any point if they think they have encountered a predator. It is never the kid's fault, so don't act like it is. Be understanding and calm about it—keep the channel open.

You can also call the school, as well as your child's best friend's parents, and make sure there are safeguards on the computers. But again, computer/device monitoring is easy to overcome, so consider a holistic approach. Working with your child's school is a great way to keep the school staff informed and active while working together to create programs and whistleblowing features that make it easy for kids to divulge if they are having problems with someone on the internet.

Although the internet has made it easier for all of us to stay connected, it has made it easier for the bad people to stay connected too. The second your kid has access to the internet, you need to lay some ground rules about potentially chatting with predators. It's a reality they must know if they have access to Google.

CHAPTER 8

Coding & The Future

Now that we've gotten the negative, scarier sides of digital immersion out of the way, it's time to look at a promising element of this new age of technology. You are now equipped with ways to keep your kids safe from the internet, as well as with strategies for keeping their personal information locked up. But what about those new services, opportunities, jobs, and completely digital languages that have emerged with this whole digital transformation?

Coding, also known as *computer language*, is the foundation of any web application, mobile application, website, algorithm, or anything else that basically makes your day move with ease. There are many different coding languages and applications, all of which can look like random numbers and letters to someone with no coding background.

Most adults today will have zero coding knowledge and, therefore, not actively encourage their child to learn more about coding and computer science in general. But that's a huge mistake. Like math, history, and English, coding is quickly becoming a mandatory skill that's just as integral to twenty-first-century education. In fact, many analysts and journalists have referred to coding as the "new literacy." Our school system is designed to teach the "old literacy" when students are young. Why can't we do the same with coding?

Research shows that the earlier we introduce skills to students, the more likely they are to retain the information and use it later in life. Not to mention, it's more cost-effective to teach these skills when students are young, as it's far more difficult to learn new skills and languages when we're older.

And for students who learn to code, there's a tremendous payoff. In 2016, the Bureau of Labor Statistics reported that the average salary for a software developer was $102,480; $79,840 for a computer programmer. The average annual earnings for all careers are just $37,040. If coding is part of a student's skill set, their earning potential will skyrocket. Furthermore, demand for coding-related jobs is only expected to increase. By 2026, 24 percent more software developers will be needed.

Of course, these benefits are related to earnings and career trajectory. But there's more to gain from coding than a six-figure salary. Kids who code will be better problem solvers, they'll have more career flexibility, and they'll be able to use coding in a wide variety of fields, not just computer science.

So though the world of coding might seem scary to parents or teachers who aren't digital connoisseurs, it pays to get your kids involved as early as possible. The internet isn't just a place for entertainment or to avoid risks. It's also a window into a productive, fruitful life, made possible with the right education and opportunities at the right age.

As we covered at the beginning of this book, coding and computer science are here to stay. If you want your kid to have a predictably lucrative future, this is one of those hobbies you should start promoting as soon as possible.

Like any foreign language, the earlier kids start to learn the basics of coding, the more fluent they will become.

Coding Basics: Which One Should My Kid Learn First?

There are different computer languages out there for different purposes. Coding isn't a one-size-fits-all solution, which is why you should know more about what's available to your kid:

1. **Python:**

   Python is generally regarded as the easiest coding language to learn. So it's typically the first one students pick when they're getting started on their adventure. Before jumping into all of the strict syntax rules, Python is a coding language that reads almost like English and is simple to understand. It's a good choice if you are new to programming. With Python, you can obtain a basic knowledge of coding practices without having to obsess over small details that become incredibly important in other languages.

   Python can help coders make websites, graphic user interfaces, and software. It was actually even used to build Instagram, YouTube, and Spotify. Since it's simpler than other languages, it's often thought of as a slower language due to the testing it requires.

2. **C:**

   C is definitely a more difficult coding language to learn, but it is still a first language pick because of all of the programming languages that are based on it, like C++ and C#. Once you learn C, it's a breeze to learn the other similar languages.

   C is often regarded as a machine-level coding language and is great for learning how a computer functions. Some programmers have compared it to understanding basic anatomy if you were to become a doctor. If you take the time to tackle this one and really get to know it, then the sky is the limit.

3. **Java:**

   Java is known as an object-oriented and feature-heavy programming language that is in seriously high demand today. If your child graduates from a Java coding boot camp, they will be in business. Java can be written on any device and is cross-platform, which means it's a highly functional coding language.

   That's why some of today's top employers of Java programmers include the likes of eBay, Amazon, and IBM. Java is also used for Android and iOS app development, which makes it the go-to coding language if you want to build mobile apps.

   At the end of the day, Java is not as easy as Python, but it is still considered a relatively user-friendly coding option. But it will take much longer to deploy your first project, and that's perfectly okay.

4. **JavaScript:**

   After Java comes JavaScript, which is the basis of most websites you visit today, as well as apps like Twitter, Gmail, Spotify, Facebook, and Instagram. This coding language is required when adding interactivity to websites since it communicates with both HTML and CSS. It is therefore essential for front-end development and consumer-facing websites. At the same time, it's becoming more and more important in backend development as well, leading the charge in test automation frameworks.

   Since JavaScript is already built into browsers, there's nothing to install, so it's considered the easiest coding language to get started with in terms of setup.

   On the downside, JavaScript is interpreted differently across browsers. And it is definitely not as easy to learn as Python. Some form of schooling or education is necessary to make this coding language accessible to your child.

5. **Ruby:**

   And last but not least, we have Ruby. Similar to Python, in that it's one of the easiest coding languages to learn without any prior programming experience, Ruby comes with a multitude of libraries and tools that make it highly versatile.

   Ruby is most sought after for its full-stake framework, Ruby on Rails. Airbnb, Grubhub, Groupon, and Soundcloud are a few examples of apps built on Ruby on Rails, proving how active its developer community has become today.

   The one criticism is that the software has a hard time performing on larger websites, which is why it's typically a desirable option for smaller websites.

Coding Bootcamps

Since so many schools are failing to deliver students with an education in coding, there are tons of coding boot camps available for kids and those who choose to ignore higher education for immediate coding deployment instead. Amazingly, these boot camps can last between fourteen and twenty-four weeks, which makes them significantly less demanding than a four-year school.

Coding bootcamps cost a lot of money. That's why, as a parent, you probably wish basic public education could just get it right the first time.

But what if you don't have the time or money for a coding boot camp? Consider finding one of the many textbooks with "Coding for Kids" in the title or consider one of the web-based coding games. These provide fun ways to teach basic coding skills. Even if your kids are not going to go into a career in coding, just being familiar with it will give them a leg up in any tech industry.

In a subsequent book, we will publish a manual your children can use to learn to code in a fun and engaging way.

CHAPTER 9

7 Reasons Why Kids Should Be Educated on Digital Developments

You've almost made it to the end of Preparing Our Kids for Digital Immersion! If you've made it this far, it means you're passionate about changing your involvement in your child's digital future. If we want to remain vigilant, protected, alert, and competitive globally, we all need to come together and change the current narrative.

We've spent a lot of time redefining how we look at this issue, but before closing out the discussion, it's important to understand these seven final reasons why kids should be educated on the digital developments and opportunities available to them today:

1. **The Tech Sector Isn't Slowing Down Anytime Soon:**

   Have you noticed how quickly new iPhones, app versions, and other gadgets are made available to our markets today? Technology isn't going to slow down for anyone. In fact, it's developing so rapidly that some people are worried about the potential of AI robots getting smarter than us within the next hundred years.

   Self-driving cars and Ubers are on the way. Drones are delivering mail. You get the picture.

   We need to expand our pool of talent as a country to seize the opportunities in front of us. Instead of lamenting the closing of big department stores, we should be shifting the focus to all of the available jobs in the tech sector. It's not that the jobs are completely gone, it is just that they're under a new title reflecting the new technical nature of them. Tech isn't going anywhere anytime soon.

2. **Students with Tech Backgrounds Earn More:**

As we have alluded to many times in this book, students with highly sought-after degrees in coding and computer science are going out into a market that is begging for applicants. Instead of watching your child wrestle with crippling student loan debt as they try to get a job with their liberal arts degree, why not put them on a path to success starting in high school?

Plus, there are many different tech specialties aside from coding and cybersecurity that students can consider learning and exploring. Or they can get a computer science degree in conjunction with another degree, like biology, and help with all of the tech-related requirements in that field. Computer skills requirements aren't just reserved for one or two industries.

3. **Tech Defense Education Will Make Students More Confident:**

Right now, students feel like they are drowning in a sea of anxiety, trying to navigate everything hard about growing up while being cyberbullied, monitored online, and stalked via predators. Preparing them with the tools, education, and know-how to navigate these waters will give them a newfound sense of confidence.

As a tech-savvy person, they will be less susceptible to unwelcome advances and predators who look for weak, vulnerable people. They will also not accept bullying and be more likely to do something about it, report the perpetrator, or tell you. Confidence goes a long, long way.

4. **Technology Is Universal:**

Students with bilingual capabilities are highly valued today. Why? Because we have entered a global marketplace, one that includes economies from around the world. In the same vein, understanding how technology, programming, and communication work will position your kid much more favorably in the hiring hierarchy.

They may even be able to work abroad!

5. **Learning Code Increases Critical Thinking Skills:**

When students learn computer science at a young age, it activates the areas of their brains that enhance their critical thinking skills. With these skills, they will excel in a variety of other subjects and become sophisticated problem solvers at a young age.

This talent will make them more confident in their ability to take on projects and tasks. It will also make them more confident people and therefore less likely to be preyed upon, as we mentioned above.

6. **Cyberattacks Are Increasing Every Day:**

The cost of cyberattacks in 2019 is expected to be double that of 2018. Cyber hackers aren't going anywhere. They are becoming so advanced that companies are opening entire cybersecurity departments just to ensure information and sensitive facts are kept private.

It's important that kids learn basic cybersecurity measures before a hacker gets to them first. It's only a matter of time.

7. **Tech Education Will Make Your Child Happier:**

So much of what we do and share is linked to technology today. It's our everything. Helping your child become a master of their technological immersion will give them self-esteem, confidence, critical thinking skills, and a bright future.

All of this, in turn, will make your child happier. They don't have to be a sitting duck in this new world of digital immersion—they can grab the bull by the horns.

CHAPTER 10

Redefining How We Look at Child Online Activity

In order for us to achieve the lasting, critical results our world and our children desperately need now and in the future, we have to reframe how we approach these topics. Making them taboo and off the table makes them secretive. When something is secretive, it promotes faulty, radical behavior or rebellion from children.

We can't pretend online predators or cyberbullies don't exist; the idyllic world you wanted for your child simply doesn't exist. However, you can prepare your child to navigate the obstacles with seamless ease and confidence. It's all about adapting to what is in front of us today.

There are a few components that I think, through proper acceptance, will help you, your community, and your teachers better approach the topic of children's online activity:

Positive Reception

Instead of speaking with a negative tone about technology and resisting it because you don't understand it or didn't grow up with it, speak about it with a positive attitude. Don't make it this big, dark, awful concept that makes your kids feel like they need to hide what they are doing online.

Change the conversation to one that is positive, so everyone feels like they can speak up. Your kids might even have a passion for learning more about the digital world and want to share more of it with you.

Constant Administration

No one said parenting or teaching was going to be easy. Even after all of this, there are still those predators out there who can really mess with your kid's head. You need to be active and follow our warning signs for determining if your child is being bullied or targeted online.

Establish clear rules that everyone follows. Don't ban technology outright, but don't sit back either. Talk with other parents and teachers to make sure there is an observance system in place.

Gamification

Last but not least: make it *fun*. All of these topics (cybersecurity, cyberbullying, social media interactions, online predators, and coding) can be taught in school with games, quizzes, hands-on learning opportunities, and even field trips. When people hear the word *code*, they assume it has to be monotonous and cringeworthy.

Through the process of gamification, we're determined to show you that these intense tech topics can be something your kids actually *want* to learn about.

This is exactly what we are doing at Security Squad. Our platform tackles this problem head-on with our suite of interactive online games designed to teach kids (K-12) all about online and privacy security, cyberbullying, and protection from negative social media interactions and online predators. Our games even dive into the world of coding to teach children how to construct their own applications. Most importantly, in everything we do, Security Squad aims to inform, protect, and prepare children to face these digital challenges with confidence.

Our gamified material makes it easy to incorporate our educational content into the classroom or at home. The material is designed specifically for teachers and parents who want to educate their children on the dangers of the online world we know today.

Conclusion

We are living in a technological world. There's no other way to describe it. If it has you overwhelmed, know that you are not alone. What's most important is that the youth of our nation feel equipped, protected, and educated when it comes to all the good and bad attached to technological development and dissemination.

We don't want you to feel alone in this fight. That's why we founded our startup.

Security Squad

We are determined to work with all stakeholders who can benefit from tech education by providing security information, support, and access to teachers, administrators, parents, and students. We bring with us a background in American security, leveraging our individual expertise to position everyone with an advanced understanding of cybersecurity, cybercriminals, and coding implementation.

We are passionate about helping you navigate these new digital waters. Just because public schools are dragging their heels doesn't mean you need to. We're another option.

Together, we're determined to change the conversation about youth education and immersion into digital topics.

Are you ready to join the movement? Get in contact with our team today.